W9-DCV-566

To:

From:

Proven Sales
Secrets to
Win Over the
Buyer's Heart
and Mind

THE
NEUROSCIENCE
of SELLING

JOHN ASHER

Award-winning author of *Close Deals Faster*

IGNITE READS
spark impact in just one hour

simple **truths**
▸ Small books. BIG IMPACT.

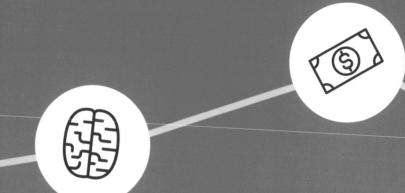

Photo Credits
Internal images © end sheets, cnythzl/Getty Images; page xi, duncan1890/Getty Images; page xii, Michael H/Getty Images; page xviii, Artur Debat/Getty Images; page 6, Maskot/Getty Images; page 12, Erik Isakson/Getty Images; page 18, 48, 51, 127, Westend61/Getty Images; page 22, B&M Noskowski/Getty Images; page 28, toxawww/Getty Images; page 34, Abdul Halim Hadi Talib/EyeEm/Getty Images; page 36, Alan Schein Photography/Getty Images; page 54, 92, 96, PeopleImages/Getty Images; page 60, Caiaimage/Paul Bradbury/Getty Images; page 62, pixelfit/Getty Images; page 67, Kerkez/Getty Images; page 72, Igor Emmerich/Getty Images; page 83, Mint Images/Getty Images; page 86, 118, Hero Images/Getty Images; page 90, Johner Images/Getty Images; page 94, Tom Werner/Getty Images; page 110, Towfiqu Photography/Getty Images; page 122, sanjeri/Getty Images; page 128, d3sign/Getty Images; page 132, pixelfit/Getty Images
Internal images on pages vi, xiv, 16, 27, 44, 52, 56, 77, 100, 104, 108, and 131 have been provided by Pexels, Pixabay, or Unsplash; these images are licensed under CC0 Creative Commons and have been released by the author for public use.

Published by Simple Truths, an imprint of Sourcebooks
P.O. Box 4410, Naperville, Illinois 60567-4410
(630) 961-3900
sourcebooks.com

Printed and bound in China.
OGP 10 9 8 7 6 5 4 3 2 1

This work is dedicated to the
ASHER SALES TEAM
who work with our prospects and
clients to close deals faster.

TABLE OF
CONTENTS

INTRODUCTION

Nothing happens until somebody sells something!

Most businesspeople will agree with this statement, and most top executives have adopted the philosophy that everyone in their company who interacts with a prospective or current customer is a salesperson. We are selling ourselves, we are selling to our managers, and our managers are selling to us. We are selling our ideas. So, almost all of us are in sales. The most productive salespeople have learned how to sell by listening to experts, reading books, learning from their mentors, and by trial and error.

Sales has always been considered an art. We know that there is also real *science* behind effective sales techniques. In the last five years, there has been an explosion of information from neuroscientists in numerous countries.[1] Most of these neuroscientists have been using functional MRI (fMRI) machines in their research, so we can now directly observe what areas of our brains are stimulated by certain actions of other people.[2]

If you were to ask these neuroscientists why they are doing these studies to measure and map brain activity, other than for academic reasons, they will say they are looking for greater insights into human communications, human relationships, and decision-making.

However, if you were to ask the same neuroscientists how their studies apply to sales, you would almost certainly get a blank stare in response, perhaps paired with the follow-up question, "What do you mean by *sales*?"

Lucky for you, ASHER Strategies has worked diligently to analyze these studies and organize the results into practical applications for executives, salespeople, and other customer-facing people. Why? To drive results in sales that lead to increased company growth. In many cases, these insights upset what many people had thought were the right techniques to use when selling to and influencing other people. In other cases, we have found new, more science-based ways to improve techniques that already exist.

The most effective salespeople use both the art *and* the science behind sales to close deals much faster than their competitors and totally disrupt what many salespeople have always been taught and believed.

Of course, understanding how this massive amount of research applies to all types of human decision-making takes a basic understanding of how the human brain functions. Let's begin by breaking down three main areas of the brain in what is known as the triune brain model.[3]

First, with the advent of vertebrates (early fish) 500 million years ago, the reptilian brain was formed. This part of the brain is the fight, flight, freeze, or appease brain. It controls all of our functions such as breathing, digestion, and heart rate. These processes happen automatically—we don't have to think about them.

Second, about 150 million years ago with the advent of mammals (whales, manatees, etc.), the mammalian brain was formed. The mammalian brain senses feelings, excitement, and engagement. It stores images, and when it sees new ones, it does pattern matching to provide input to decisions.

Finally, about 2 to 3 million years ago with the evolution of primates, including humans, the hominid brain came on the scene. It assesses facts, figures, and logic and can understand complex concepts.

For simplicity's sake, since both are more than 150 million years old, the reptilian and mammalian sections

FIGURE: THE OLD BRAIN MAKES THE DECISIONS

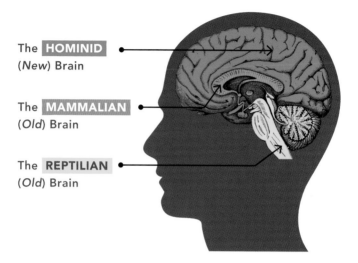

The **HOMINID** (*New*) Brain

The **MAMMALIAN** (*Old*) Brain

The **REPTILIAN** (*Old*) Brain

of the brain are referred to together as the old brain, and the hominid brain is referred to as the new brain.

Where are almost all of our daily decisions made? You may have heard the saying "we decide on emotion and justify with logic." We now have the research to prove this statement is true. Dr. Hanna Damasio, previously of the University of Lisbon and now of the University of Southern California, studied people

whose old brains were damaged from disease or injury. These people could not make simple decisions. They could not even decide whether to have a ham or turkey sandwich for lunch, proving that the old brain decides, not the hominid brain.

Therefore, buyers buy on emotion and justify with logic. Here is a practical example of how it applies to sales:

Many salespeople think the only necessary requirement to get the sale is to offer great products and services...but that is not enough. You must also have a great relationship with the buyer. For example, your company and two other companies are vying for a large opportunity with a buyer. All three companies have great logical information, relevant experience, great quality and service, and reasonable prices. In the buyer's mind, all three companies are tied for first with their logical solutions. Which one does the buyer choose?

The buyer's old brain decides based on how it feels

about the companies, including which seller has made the strongest emotional connection by building the best rapport.

Here is how logic comes into play. If one of the three companies vying for the job scores significantly lower than the other two based on experience, quality, service, and prices, the buyer will not pick that company even if its salesperson has built the strongest relationship. The buyer's old brain will not choose the inferior solution, as the seller does not have the logic to justify the emotional sale.

Wouldn't it be nice to know how to get the buyer to use their old brain and choose you based on emotion?

Based on hundreds of studies at numerous major neuroscience laboratories and universities, we know the decision-making old brain responds to six main activators.[4]

1 ME ME ME Focus

2 Simple, Easy-to-Grasp Ideas

3 Beginnings and Endings

4 Clear Distinction

5 Vivid Images

6 Active Engagement

These six activators apply to getting someone's attention; therefore, they are most useful in sales presentations and customer communications. They also can be helpful in every phase of the sales process and will be mentioned throughout this book. Chapter 1 gives you all the details.

In a closely related field, neuroscientists, psychologists, and various researchers have identified over one hundred cognitive biases.[5] Although there is no agreement on exactly how many there are, we've researched these cognitive biases and know many of them are not only useful for marketing, but also have great value and practical applications for sales. This book shows how understanding twenty-five specific cognitive biases can help you be more effective in five of the most important sales skills:[6]

▶ *Prospecting for New Business*
▶ *Identifying Buyers and Using Coaches*
▶ *Rapport Building*

▸ *Perfect Listening*

▸ *Closing the Deal*

The importance of cognitive biases in the sales process is covered in chapter 2, and their uses are explained in the subsequent chapters dedicated to each important sales skill.

The Neuroscience of Selling takes some of the mystery out of how and why people buy, and it better enables you to connect to any buyer and close deals faster. These insights are useful for business executives, salespeople, and all other customer-facing associates. That's what we do best at ASHER Strategies: make the complex simple with practical applications so you can bring in new clients and grow your business.

CHAPTER

ONE

Six Activators That Wake Up the Buyer's Brain

Almost all decisions are made by the buyer's decision-making old brain, but if the old brain remains asleep, the buyer will not make a decision, and your closing rates will be close to zero.

Activators

Use the following six old brain activators to increase your chances for a sale:

1. ME ME ME Focus

We are all most concerned with our own safety, our own happiness, and our own success. This is our reptilian brain at work, and one practical application of this activator you can easily recognize is in sales presentations. When you watch most salespeople give a presentation to buyers, it is all about the salesperson's company and the company's offerings. The typical agenda of their presentation looks like this:

▸ *Here is the vision of our company.*

▸ *Here is a picture of our new facilities.*

▸ *Here are all of our locations around the country.*

▸ *Here is a list of our seven integrated cybersecurity solutions.*

▸ *Let's start with the details of our first solution.*

Is the buyer's brain awake yet? Not a chance! So, how do *elite* salespeople start a presentation?

Using research, their referral source, or an inside coach, they start their presentations with an understanding of the *customer needs.*

Studies of buyer behavior with fMRI machines show that in 95 percent of the cases, a description of the buyer's needs will cause an immediate conversation between the buyer and the seller.[7] Now, we have the buyer's decision-making old brain immediately awake and engaged with us. The buyer's old brain lights up like a Christmas tree!

PRACTICAL APPLICATION

Always start your presentation with an understanding of the customer's needs.

Last year, I was in Toronto delivering a sales presentation to fifteen CEOs in the small- and medium-sized business market. One of the CEOs was a young woman running a full-service digital marketing agency, and when I mentioned the importance of starting presentations with the customer needs, she leaned forward in her seat and began to speak!

"Wow, I have a presentation tomorrow with the largest telecom company in Ontario," she said enthusiastically. "There are four firms presenting to a group of senior buyers. The other three companies are large; one of them is the incumbent, and they have had the job for four years. I'm pretty sure they invited me so that they can 'check the box' that they talked to a small business… What do I have to lose?" she continued with a broad smile. "I'm going to blow up my presentation and start with my understanding of their needs. I know what they are."

"Great! Let me know how it goes," I answered.

She emailed me two days later and was extremely excited to share that she had won the opportunity. Eureka!

Another example of the first old brain activator (ME ME ME Focus) is the answer to this question: Are buyers' decision-making old brains stimulated by listening to salespeople talk? Hardly.

Most salespeople have learned one of the key selling skills is to *listen* to the customer. In fact, many sales trainers advise that we should use our mouth and ears in the proportion that the man upstairs gave them to us. That is, listen twice as much as we talk.

Studies with fMRI machines show when we engage with another person to talk about what they are really interested in (e.g., their background, their needs, their passion, their company, etc.), more positive hormones (dopamine, serotonin, and oxytocin) are released in their brain than when making money, falling in love, or eating a great meal![8]

Therefore, before interacting with another person (buyer, banker, channel partner, etc.), thoroughly research them. Use websites (e.g., LinkedIn) and social media to thoroughly know them so you can get them talking about what they love to talk about. They'll feel great, and their old brains will transfer these great feelings to you.

2. Simple, Easy-to-Grasp Ideas

The second old brain activator is Simple, Easy-to-Grasp Ideas. Our hominid brain can understand all kinds of complex concepts, but the decision-making old brain cannot.

When a salesperson says, "We have a flexible, integrated, and scalable solution with fifteen exit waypoints," the buyer's new brain thinks, *Great!*

But how about the buyer's old brain? The old brain is totally confused. It does not hear words, facts, or figures. Will a confused brain make a decision? *No!*

The practical application of the second old brain activators is one we all know: keep it simple.

Last year, I participated in the annual meeting of the Human Capital Management Association in Las Vegas, and I had some time to look around between keynotes. There were about twenty vendors that had set up ten-by-ten-foot booths in the convention center meeting room.

Here is some very easy advice on how to design a trade show booth: keep it simple.

As the average person approaches your booth, they look at it for an average of three seconds.[9] You want a qualified lead to look at your booth and in less than three seconds decide they want to come in and talk to you.

You want a nonqualified lead to look at your booth and in less than three seconds decide they do not need your products and services and keep walking. You do not want them to come in and waste your time and perhaps divert your attention from a qualified prospect.

So, I walked around and looked at all the booths, most of which cost the vendors about $10,000 for the three days. Every single one of them was too complicated! One supplier had seventeen different services listed on the front column.

> **PRACTICAL APPLICATION**
>
> Consider simplifying the descriptions of your products and services everywhere—in your presentations, proposals, brochures, and on your website.

3. Beginnings and Endings

The third old brain activator is about the importance of the Beginnings and Endings of interactions. If properly stimulated, the old brain will wake up at the beginning of a meeting, conversation, or presentation, but once the old brain gets the gist of the idea, it goes to sleep. If stimulated again near the end of the interaction, it will wake up once more.

An example of this activator is a typical sermon given by pastors, priests, and rabbis, who are all taught in theological seminary how to give an impactful message.

1. Describe an important story from the Bible with enthusiasm. The congregation leans forward on the edge of their pews! Their old brains are awake!

2. Elaborate with detailed background information in the body of the sermon. The congregation's old brains are lulled to sleep.

3. Near the end of the sermon, show how the biblical story relates to the daily lives of the congregation. Their old brains wake back up!

This pattern is also well-known in the entertainment industry. In *Star Wars*, George Lucas's first film in the franchise that came out in 1977, Lucas went against Hollywood protocol of starting with the credits and instead started with action and the crawler, "A long time ago in a galaxy far, far away..." The movie ended in classic adventure style, with the good guys winning and wrongs being righted. The formula works: have a hot opening and a hot closing and try not to mess up the middle!

PRACTICAL APPLICATION

In every interaction with a prospect or customer—whether it is an email, a phone call, or a meeting in person—always begin and end with impact.

4. Clear Distinction

The fourth old brain activator is about Clear Distinction. The old brain remains fast asleep when presented with similar boring patterns. The old brain loves bright, shiny, stark differences. For example:

"We are one of the leading companies in this industry." (The old brain yawns.)

"Our company has unique testing facilities." (The old brain wakes up!)

If a seller says, "We've been in business for thirty-five years. We have great customer service. We have a strong engineering and design team," the buyer's hominid brain hears only three things: "Blah blah blah."

Why does the hominid brain only hear "Blah blah blah"? Because while most salespeople think these are key discriminators, they actually do not differentiate you from the competition. In most cases, statements like these are the price of admission in today's globalized, internet-based economy; you must have them to be considered. To wake up the buyer's old brain with this activator, you must be different.

The best way to show the buyer's old brain a clear difference is to have a unique selling proposition (USP)

highlighting a benefit for your product or service that makes it unique. If you do, the buyer's old brain can make a quick decision. To show this clear distinction, you must use words such as "unique," "only," and "top-rated." Additionally, not only must it be different from your competition, but it also must be relevant to your buyer.

For example, our company has the following two USPs:

First, we are the only global sales training company where every trainer is a former CEO.

This USP accounts for half of the new business we get. Many CEOs would like it if their sales trainer wasn't just a trainer but was also able to understand all areas of business, including marketing, engineering, operations, and human resources.

Second, we are the only global sales training company where every trainer has a technical or marketing background.

As the world becomes more technical, this USP

is extremely relevant to many buyers. Many CEOs of technical companies would like their sales trainer to have credibility with technical salespeople.

PRACTICAL APPLICATION

Develop a *USP* for your company. The buyer will understand your company is unique and will make the easy decision to choose you.

There is an additional practical application of the reason to have a strong USP. If you do not have a USP, buyers don't see a significant difference between your company and your competition. Therefore, most buyers will keep looking, and your sales process becomes stalled. Or the buyer's old brain will view your offering as a commodity and will start negotiating your prices.

For companies selling a pure commodity, it may be difficult to develop a USP. Diesel oil would be an example where the buyer only really cares about price and availability. In this case, the second-best approach to wake up the buyer's old decision-making brain with the

Clear Distinction activator is to develop a WHY for your company.

Many of us would like to do business with a company that has a compelling why. Simon Sinek was the first to popularize this idea in his widely followed TED Talk, "Start with Why." He says:

"Every company can describe what they do. Every company can describe how they do it. Very few companies can describe why they do what they do."

In cases where companies can clearly describe why they do what they do (sometimes described as the company's purpose), they can better connect with prospects and customers. As a relevant example, the why for our company is *making the complex simple.* You can see the ASHER WHY at work as you read this book!

5. Vivid Images

The fifth old brain activator is about Vivid Images. Written words have little influence on the old brain.

The old brain only stores images/pictures and uses them for pattern matching when it sees new images. Facts and figures often have less impact.

Videos—which are really just a series of pictures—can be powerful sales tools. At the end of a recent Institute for Excellence in Sales keynote speech I gave on the subject of using videos, a CEO came up to chat. She said, "I love your ideas about the importance of videos. I understand their power for companies selling products, but I'm a service provider, so I'm not really sure what videos I could make."

I shared a couple of websites for service providers who have done a great job with videos so she could see some examples. Three months later, she emailed me with a link to her website with videos that she and her team had developed. They were great! I asked her if they were helping her closing rates. She replied, "Last month my closing rates essentially doubled from 23 percent to 41 percent."

Here is another example. We have a client who is

a commercial insurance broker. Its staff act as brokers between companies who need commercial insurance, which comes in four distinct types, and large insurance companies who provide the insurance policies. Many of their ongoing customers would be using the brokers for two of the four lines of insurance. When their customers would need a third line of insurance, their CFOs would routinely go get their own quotes from insurances companies worldwide instead of going through their broker.

After hearing their frustrations, I suggested that they make a one-minute video of what they do and show it to their current customers. They did. When the brokers showed the video, the universal reaction was, "Oh! That's what you do!" Customers' old brains were able to comprehend the video much more quickly than the company's traditional brochures.

PRACTICAL APPLICATION

Use the power of video. Wake up the buyer's old brain with self-explanatory pictures and videos in your presentations, in your proposals, and on your website.

6. Active Engagement

The sixth old brain activator is about Active Engagement. We know from fMRI studies that there are many ways to stimulate the buyer's old brain with an emotional customer story.[10] As the buyer's old brain listens to your story about how you have made another company like theirs successful, their old brain releases three positive hormones—dopamine, serotonin, and oxytocin (the so-called "happy chemicals")—and starts to identify with your story.

Here is an example of a customer story I recently related to a prospect:

We recently worked with a company just like yours. The sales manager told us sales had been stagnant for three years. We started by analyzing the sales aptitude of their people, which was average. Over the next six months, we helped them upgrade their sales force to a group with a superior aptitude for sales. After a year, their sales had increased by 30 percent, with two-thirds the number of salespeople as before. Gross margin, therefore, increased by 70 percent.

As the prospect was about halfway through listening to my customer story, I could tell his old brain was feeling like it was actually in the story. At the end of the story, it was apparent that his old brain was exclaiming, *Wow! I wonder if I could get those same results!*

PRACTICAL APPLICATION

Use stories about your customer successes with other customers. The great salespeople are the great storytellers.

Place videos on your website of your best customers telling the stories of how you and your company have made them successful. This is a terrific application of combining the power of video with the emotion generated by a customer story.

In the next chapter, we will continue to build neuroscience sales skills with cognitive biases.

CHAPTER
TWO

Cognitive Biases in the Sales Process

Our brains are very complex organs. They contain one hundred billion neurons, and each neuron has ten thousand connections or synapses. For our brains to make complex decisions, it takes a lot of energy. Therefore, over hundreds of millions of years, our brains have learned to save that energy by developing shortcuts, snap judgments, and rules of thumb to quickly make adequate decisions based on a limited amount of information. These shortcuts are called cognitive biases—the tendency of people to perceive their environment based on their experiences and preferences.[11]

A simple example is smoke. When our brains sense smoke, we immediately think there is a high probability that a fire is causing the smoke. Our brains are being helpful in warning us of potential danger.

Cognitive biases are helpful when speed and efficiency are needed in decision-making, but in some cases, a bias can lead us down the wrong path. In this instance, the cognitive bias is called a **heuristic**. An example is stereotyping.

In the early 1980s, I founded an engineering company. We needed a software developer with special skills in the engineering of signal processing systems to support a U.S. Navy acoustic development program. It was a high-priority job for the U.S. Navy, but the top candidate for the job was not recommended by our HR director.

When the candidate had the face-to-face interview with her, she was shut down by his appearance, which included the following:

- *Ball cap on backward*
- *T-shirt of a rapper group known for using four-letter words*
- *Untrimmed mustache and beard*
- *Unbuttoned long-sleeved shirt hanging out*
- *Dirty tennis shoes*

Our HR director's old brain rejected the candidate based solely on his appearance, but because of the candidate's outstanding qualifications, our director of engineering insisted on interviewing the candidate and immediately hired him. He had just the right qualifications and experience to get the job done for our client.

Luckily for us, our director of engineering did not let the stereotyping cognitive bias get in the way of this important decision. The new employee turned out to be terrific. His outstanding work on many of our contracts resulted in a continuous flow of business over a decade.

My book *Close Deals Faster* describes in detail the top ten selling skills I developed to help salespeople bring in new clients in a more structured and systematic way.[12] The next chapters cover the five most important of these sales skills and include neuroscience-based practical applications:

1. Prospecting for New Business

2. Identifying Buyers and Using Coaches

3. Rapport Building

4. Perfect Listening

5. Closing the Deal

All five skills apply to salespeople, the last four apply to executives, and the middle three apply to all customer-facing people.

As we proceed through these important sales skills, knowledge of twenty-five cognitive biases that apply to sales will provide valuable input not only for your customer interactions but also for interactions with your sales managers and other company associates.

CHAPTER

THREE

Prospecting for New Business

The objective of prospecting is to identify and qualify new leads who can eventually be turned into customers. Prospecting is a fundamental key to sales success. Both companies and salespeople are involved in prospecting for new business leads.

Here are the typical ways that companies develop leads:

- *Outsourcing through a telemarketing company to generate leads*
- *Internet technologies (SEO/SEM), email blast campaigns, blogs, content-rich websites, marketing automation, and customer relationship management (CRM) systems*
- *Direct mail*
- *Trade shows*
- *Using inside salespeople (cold callers)*
- *Analyzing current customers and developing account-based marketing programs (marketing to prospects similar to their current customers)*

Here are typical ways that salespeople develop leads:

- *Cold calling*
- *Asking for—and following up on—referrals*
- *Networking*
- *Using social media tools*

Qualifying Leads

If your company turns highly qualified leads over to you as a salesperson, great! Unfortunately, that's not usually the case. To properly qualify a lead, you need answers to these questions:

▶ *Does this prospect fit the profile of our ideal customer group (i.e., your dream clients)? For example, does your product or service fit your target audience and buyers in size, location, services, etc.?*

▶ *Does this prospect have a critical or urgent need?*

▶ *Do we know what results (key performance indicators [KPIs]) the customer wants?*

▶ *Do we have a coach ("insider") in or close to the customer's organization?*

▶ *Is solving this need in the prospect's budget?*

▶ *Has a purchasing time frame been established?*

▶ *Have we identified the right decision-makers who have the authority to buy (e.g., user, technical, and economic buyers)?*

- *Do we have a potential solution to satisfy their need?*

- *Are the projected revenues and margins sufficient for us?*

- *Are their credit history and current financial condition stable?*

- *Is this a buyer we want as a customer, or is the buyer too much trouble?*

There are a number of cognitive biases that apply to the qualification of leads—the availability bias, the false consensus bias, the choice-supportive bias, the optimism bias, and the sunk cost bias. Let's learn how they can help you qualify leads and make sure that they remain qualified.

Biases

The Availability Bias

The availability bias is a mental shortcut that causes us to rely only on immediate examples that come to mind when evaluating a specific topic, concept, method, or decision. We make decisions based on the knowledge readily available in our minds rather than examining all the alternatives. This bias gives our brains a quick shortcut to the answer needed.

PRACTICAL APPLICATION

Be careful not to assume a lead is qualified with a limited amount of data.

The False Consensus Bias

The false consensus bias occurs when people tend to overestimate the extent to which their opinions, beliefs, preferences, values, and habits are normal and typically related to those of others. We assume other people think and feel as we do.

PRACTICAL APPLICATION

Be open to other opinions about everything. Frequently discuss the qualification status of your top prospects with your sales manager.

The Choice-Supportive Bias

The choice-supportive bias comes into play after we make a decision. When we choose something, we tend to feel positive about it, even if the choice has flaws. We buy a dog. We think our dog is awesome even if it bites people once in a while. People tend to trust any piece of information that supports their choice. We can be blind to information that opposes the choice we made or a strongly held belief.

PRACTICAL APPLICATION

Pay particular attention to new information that would indicate the lead is no longer qualified.

The Optimism Bias

The optimism bias causes us to believe we are at a lesser risk of experiencing a negative outcome compared to a positive one. Our old brain tends to make us more optimistic than we should be (wishful thinking). We are wired to believe the future will be better.

PRACTICAL APPLICATION

If the sales process with a lead has gone radio silent for two weeks (no response to your inquiries), it is no longer qualified (e.g., a buying decision is not imminent). In many cases, it means that one of your competitors has an inside "coach." Clear it from your active pipeline.

The Sunk Cost Bias

The sunk cost bias is our tendency to irrationally pursue an activity that is not meeting our expectations because of the time and/or money we have already spent on it. We stick with opportunities too long when we have already invested a lot. "We can't give up on this opportunity. I've been working on it for nine months! I'm sure that it will close soon."

PRACTICAL APPLICATION

Don't let sunk costs affect your decision concerning whether the lead remains qualified.

Lead Management

Once a lead is identified and qualified, it must be managed to turn it into a customer. Often, a lot of follow-up is needed to transform leads into customers. There are two cognitive biases that apply to lead management and follow-up—the familiarity bias and the reciprocity bias.

The Familiarity Bias

The familiarity bias comes into play when the familiar is favored over novel places, people, or things, despite the seemingly obvious gains from something new. Therefore, we are biased favorably toward messages that are frequently received. We judge them as safe. For example, we are influenced by media ad campaigns that appeal to our interests.

PRACTICAL APPLICATION

Repetitive touches on qualified leads are essential to sales success.

The Reciprocity Bias

The reciprocity bias describes the impulse to reciprocate to others for what they have done for us. When we give something to another person, their old brain feels obliged to reciprocate. Reciprocity is a social norm and potent motivator of relationship-building behavior. The term "much obliged" means the other person is driven to give back to you.

PRACTICAL APPLICATION

In every interaction, give something extra. Add useful content in all interactions. At the first meeting, bring the potential buyer a gift (e.g., book, prop, blog article). They will reciprocate with increased responsiveness and greater willingness to discuss their challenges.

Follow-Up

Significant effort is needed to manage the lead and follow up. It takes an average of twelve touches to make the sale to a *qualified* lead in business-to-business (B2B) sales.[13] This is the familiarity bias in action. Unfortunately, the average salesperson only makes three touches before they quit and move on.

As you can see from the follow-up ("nurture") data from the National Sales Execution Association for B2B sales, the closing rate is only 5 percent when salespeople quit after the third touch.

TOUCH #	% CLOSE
1	2%
3	5%
5–11	80%

Here is what can count as a touch on a qualified lead:

▸ *Social media contact*

▸ *Personal visit*

▸ *Email exchange*

▸ *Personal, written note*

▸ *Phone conversation*

▸ *Webinar*

▸ *Copies of interesting articles*

▸ *Trade show*

▸ *Voicemail message*

▸ *Newsletters*

▸ *Networking event*

▸ *Text message*

Based on research from the Harvard Business School and others, of the twelve touches required to make the sale to a qualified B2B lead, the average lead requires *seven* quality touches prior to the closing of the sale.[14] Only these three interactions count as a quality touch:

- *Face-to-face meeting*
- *Discussion on the phone*
- *An active electronic exchange (email/text messaging/LinkedIn/Facebook)*

You should always set an objective for the next touch (call/meeting/email). The objective is your wish for the outcome of the touch. Most of the time the objective is *not* closing the sale—it is an agreement from your lead to take the next step in the sales process.

Always conclude an interaction with an action item for yourself, even if you have to suggest it, such as, "Would you like me to send you the results after the next test of our new product?"

Within twenty-four hours of the quality touch, send an email to your lead with these four items:

- *Thank them for the meeting or phone conversation.*
- *Provide a summary of their needs that you discovered in the conversation.*
- *Remind them of the information they agreed to send to you.*
- *List the action items that you took away from the meeting.*

Sixty-six percent of buyers indicate that "consistent and relevant communication" provided by both the company's sales and marketing organizations was a key influence in choosing that company as their solution partner.[15]

The rule of thumb for touch frequency is once a month (less for very short sales cycles). Use customer relationship management (CRM) platforms to manage your touches. Provide useful content at every touch. (The reciprocity bias in action!)

Here are the reasons it takes so many touches to close a new deal:

- *It takes time for the prospect to feel totally comfortable with you, your product/service, and your organization.*
- *Their company's internal decision-making process. You may have to get a yes from multiple decision-makers.*
- *You have to displace an incumbent. They need time to assess other offers.*
- *Other reasons include changing economic conditions, management changing their priorities, major weather events, or their bank will no longer finance the deal.*

If you ask elite salespeople how many touches they will make on a qualified lead before they quit and move on, will they give you a number? No! Their attitude is, if it is qualified, they are going to pursue the lead until the buyer "buys" or "dies!" (Or gives the business to another salesperson.)

Email Follow-Up Techniques

The familiarity bias is very important in email follow-up techniques. Elite salespeople manage a consistent flow of information to prospects. *Use short emails.* Do not send everything in the first email, or there will be no reason to reach out to the prospects in the future. They are typically busy and need time to process your information. Contact them far more frequently than you think you should. As a qualified lead, they will reward your professional persistence.

Only 24 percent of sales emails are opened and read.[16] Therefore, use creative email subject lines with new information in the body of the email. These types of emails are particularly useful when you are not getting a response and you know you should be.

- *10 minutes?*
- *September 15 meeting*
- *Dogged persistence*
- *Did we miss the mark?*

- *Great picture of you in the ...*
- *Are you still alive?*
- *Quick update*

Put all of your content in the body of the email. Few people read attachments.

Use video links (Old Brain Activator #5—Vivid Images). Keep videos short (under one minute). Mention the subject of the video, the length of the video, and why they should view it in your email or social media post.

Add value with each subsequent touch, and they will look forward to hearing from you again. Courteous, professional persistence with a strong unique selling proposition (Old Brain Activator #4—Clear Distinction) will win you their attention.

CHAPTER

FOUR

Identifying Buyers and Using Coaches

After you have identified leads and qualified them, you are off and running to turn the leads into customers. The question now is, who in their organization can make the decision to buy? You can greatly increase your probability of success if you have identified exactly who the real decision-makers are and have connected with an internal coach.

The Old Brain Activator #4—Clear Distinction comes into play in this skill and four cognitive biases,

THE NEUROSCIENCE OF SELLING

one of which—reciprocity—was covered in the previous chapter.

Buyers Biases

The Likability Bias

We are biased toward others who have qualities or features that cause us to regard them favorably. Examples of these qualities include:

- *Nice*
- *Courteous*
- *Polite*
- *Adaptable*
- *Smiling*
- *Thoughtful*
- *Upbeat in tone*

- *Confident*
- *Respectful*
- *Positive*
- *Enthusiastic*
- *Well-dressed and groomed*

A sure way to engage the likability bias is to always address people by their name. British Airways boosted its customer satisfaction ratings 60 percent by having employees frequently address customers courteously by name.

PRACTICAL APPLICATION

Demonstrate the qualities of a likable person.

The Safety Bias

For the buyer, the prospect of pain (engaging in the buying process) is a much more powerful de-motivator than the promise of gain. Therefore, the buyer's old brain does not perceive most salespeople as safe.

PRACTICAL APPLICATION

Build relationships with buyers so that they feel safe with you. Treat them with respect, explain everything thoroughly, and do not pressure them for a decision until they are ready to make one.

The Trust Bias

Honesty and integrity are key factors in a decision to trust someone. If we feel someone is honest (transparent, open, and dependable) and has integrity (courage to say and do the right things and to do what they say they will do), our trust and confidence in them increases.

PRACTICAL APPLICATION

(1) Always tell the truth; (2) do what you say you will do, the way it should be done, and on time. In the sales process, most buyers will trust a salesperson if they are honest and have integrity, but they also must have strong product knowledge and the resultant power and confidence to help the buyer.

Identifying Buyers

In most sales there are three types of buyers:

1 The **user buyer** selects a seller to help them get their job done. These are the people who will use your product or service in their work. The user buyer wants to know, "Does your offering respond to my needs?"

2 The **technical buyer** gives technical approval. These can be heads of departments, engineering, and review staff. The technical buyer wants to know, "Does your solution meet our specifications/requirements?"

3 The **economic buyer** approves the money transfer to your company. These buyers can be the CEO, CFO, or purchasing manager. The economic buyer wants to know, "What kind of return will I get on the investment?"

It is important to identify these buyers as you may have to get a yes from all three. In a smaller or short sales cycle, one person may function as two of the three buyers or even all three.

Using Coaches

The most important buyer is your coach. A **coach**, also known as an *insider* or *champion*, is a person inside the prospective company who is helping you close the deal. These coaches are not sales coaches in your own organization, and you do not pay them. They like and trust you, and your products and services, and want you to help their companies.

Your coach acts like a sports coach, giving you the information you need to know to close the deal. A coach typically provides you with needs and requirements, budget, timing, decision-makers, likely competitors, influencers, internal politics, satisfaction level with the incumbent, and personality types of buyers.

The user buyer is usually the best possible coach, because they will be using your product or service daily. It's difficult to win a competition without their support, and, of course, it is useful to have multiple coaches.

The criteria for great coaches are as follows:

1. They are usually someone inside the prospect's organization, they are credible with the prospect's organization, or they work closely with the organization (e.g., banker, vendor, consultant, accountant, subcontractor, channel partner, etc.).

2. They are knowledgeable of the organization's requirements.

3. They are a person with whom you have credibility.

4. They want you to get the business.

For many salespeople, the concept of a coach helping win the sale is intuitive, but it's helpful to see the data behind it. We have found that:

▸ *If you have an inside coach, you have an 80 percent chance of getting the sale.*

- *If you do not have an inside coach, you have a 20 percent chance of getting the sale.*
- *A typical Pareto principle applies (80/20 rule).*

When you are pursuing an opportunity where you have an inside coach, there is a clear distinction between you and the competitors without a coach: the fourth old brain activator, Clear Distinction, at work again.

If you have a "must pursue" opportunity and you need a coach to help, there are a number of ways to find one:

- *Use LinkedIn first-level connections to identify potential coaches.*
- *Ask your current customers if they can make a connection for you.*
- *Ask your vendors, suppliers, consultants, and channel partners the same question.*
- *Send an email to everyone in your company: "Who knows someone in XYZ company?"*

▸ *Join forces with a salesperson from another company while avoiding direct competition (be each other's coach): "You get me into your FedEx account, and in turn, I'll get you into my Johnson & Johnson account."*

▸ *Build relationships with salespeople in your prospect's organization. Even if they do not know you, they will usually take your call. Invite them to lunch. Build a relationship with them. Turn them into your inside coaches!*

As you can see, there are two cognitive biases at work here, including the reciprocity bias (you buy them lunch and they might give you information on how to sell to their company's buyer) and the likability bias (to build this relationship, you must have the attributes of a likeable person).

Rapport Building

The rapport building skill applies to salespeople, executives, and, when you really think about it, all of us who want to be successful in life. Building rapport with a buyer involves thoroughly researching them so you have something of interest to talk about, making a good first impression, identifying their personality style so you can adapt your style to theirs, encouraging them to talk first, and keeping them talking.

Two of the decision-making old brain activators

apply to this skill: ME ME ME Focus and Vivid Images. Four cognitive biases that apply were covered previously: reciprocity, safety, trust, and likability. Eight new cognitive biases are particularly helpful in forming first impressions and building rapport.

Relationship Biases

Primacy Bias

The first impression principle is based on the primacy bias, which is the tendency for the first few things we notice about someone to influence how we interpret information about them later.

When you are with prospects and clients, you are "on stage." Your appearance should signal confidence, success, expertise, sensitivity, professionalism, and attention to detail. When people dress more casually, they tend to act more casually and less professionally.

PRACTICAL APPLICATION

Dress the way the buyer expects you to look based on its industry, geographical area, and company.

Ultimate Attribution Bias

The ultimate attribution bias arises as a way to explain the negative behavior of a person not part of your group as flaws in their personality. It is also the belief that positive acts performed by a member of your group are a result of their personality, whereas if a person in your group behaves negatively, it is a result of situational factors.

PRACTICAL APPLICATION

We are biased toward our own groups. Because buyers come from many groups other than our own (gender, age, ethnic background, etc.), be careful not to stereotype them and lose opportunities for connection and cooperation.

Confirmation Bias

The confirmation bias is the tendency to search for, interpret, favor, and recall information in a way that confirms our preexisting beliefs or hypotheses. We display this bias when we gather or remember information selectively, or when we interpret it in a biased way.

> **PRACTICAL APPLICATION**
>
> First impressions are made quickly, and it's almost impossible to change an unfavorable one. When first meeting a buyer, pay attention to your words, tone of voice, and even your body language and what you are wearing.

Physical Attraction Bias

The physical attraction bias is a tendency to assume that people who are physically attractive also possess other socially desirable personality traits.

Buyers unconsciously (old brain) use your appearance to make inferences and draw conclusions quickly. Can you sell an expensive car wearing cheap, unshined shoes? No! The buyer's old brain screams, "Warning: Incongruity!" and starts looking for other mismatches, this time in your sales offering.

> **PRACTICAL APPLICATION**
>
> Pay strict attention to your grooming, posture, and dress.

Similarity Bias

We naturally want to surround ourselves with people we feel are similar to us (safe). This similarity bias extends to all aspects of the other person—their age, gender, sports preferences, political leanings, and ethnicity. As a result, we tend to want to work with people who are like us.

PRACTICAL APPLICATION

1. Find similarities with them in their backgrounds using thorough research.
2. Dress similar to the way the other person is dressed (ask your coach for advice).
3. Use similar body language (neuro-linguistic programming techniques).

Warmth Bias

In social psychology, all interpersonal impressions tend to form along two dimensions: warmth and competence.

Our appraisals of the warmth of another person have a greater impact on our interpersonal and intergroup relations than our appraisals of their competence.

PRACTICAL APPLICATION

When you first meet someone, make solid eye contact. Maintaining good eye contact denotes attention, concentration, and true concern for what they are saying. Make it and keep it. Poor eye contact signals potential lying, unease, and/or untrustworthiness.

Physical Touch Bias

Touch is the first of our senses to develop and remains emotionally central throughout our lives. When connecting with others, there is no greater power. A good, firm handshake is a sign of both strength and mutual respect. Strangers form a better impression of those who offer their hand in greeting. It is the only time when we are socially expected to touch each other.

Having a firm handshake is extremely important for both men and women. If men get a weak handshake from another man, their old brain thinks, *Wimp!* If men get a weak handshake from a woman, their old brain thinks, *Weak!* Not surprisingly, women feel the same way about weak handshakes from men. Make your handshakes firm, but not too firm, and don't forget to smile.

PRACTICAL APPLICATION

Shake hands as many times as possible, including when first meeting the buyer, when agreeing on something during the meeting, and when walking out of the buyer's office.

With current customers use handshakes, pats on the back, fist bumps, and high fives, as appropriate.

Compliment Bias

People are more likely to be persuaded to say "yes" to your suggestions and proposals when you make them feel good about themselves. A genuine compliment at the beginning of a meeting sets a positive tone for the discussions.

PRACTICAL APPLICATION

1. Do research on the buyer's company and compliment the buyer early in the conversation about a video you watched on their website, their website layout, their facilities, their products, or even how you were treated by the company's receptionist.

2. Compliment the buyer before asking for assistance. "I am sure you know a lot about this situation. Could you share some details?"

Researching the Buyer Prior to the First Meeting

When meeting the buyer for the first time, most average salespeople will do most of the talking. The buyer's old brain is *not* stimulated when listening to salespeople talk. When first engaging with the buyer, get them to talk about themselves. This is the first old brain activator (ME ME ME Focus) at work.

Elite salespeople encourage the buyer to talk first. They do this by thoroughly researching the buyer and having them talk about what they want to talk about by asking open-ended questions. Examples of items that will motivate other people to start talking include their professional passions, how they got their job, how they started their company, their technical background, organizations they belong to, etc.

PRACTICAL APPLICATION

Use web-based sources to thoroughly research the buyer so you can get them talking about what they want to talk about. In conversations with the buyer, use the word *you* frequently.

In your research, including the Sales Navigator level on LinkedIn and through your coach, learn about the buyer's personality style, how to write an email to them, and how to deal with them in person.

First Impressions

Once we have formed a first impression of another person, that impression is anchored in our old brains. If we receive new information that confirms our initial impression, we acknowledge it. If we receive information that would change our mind about the person, we tend to reject the information. This tendency is the confirmation bias at work.

We know from neuroscience studies with fMRI machines that first impressions can be formed by the decision-making old brain in as little as a tenth of a second.[17] This extremely fast first impression was developed when the first primates saw another primate in the wild and needed to make a quick decision: *Friend? Enemy? Potential partner?* Our old brain (subconscious) makes up its mind before our rational (conscious) brain has had a chance to think about it!

There has been extensive research on how the hominid brain determines a positive or negative first impression about another person when first meeting them. One widely known study done at UCLA by Dr. Albert Mehrabian showed people make decisions about other people based on:

▸ *Verbal (what you say) (7%)*

▸ *Vocal (how you sound) (38%)*

▸ *Visual (how you look) (55%)*

Part of the first impression is made from the words that come out of our mouth (7%) when first meeting someone. Elite salespeople prepare opening statements and match words to the occasion and to whom they are speaking (e.g., executive-level words for executives, technical words for technical buyers, etc.). Tone of voice is more important (38%). Sincerity (or lack thereof) is detected immediately. Tonality is especially critical in phone conversations where there are no visuals.

It is how you look—including body language—that carries the most weight in an initial person-to-person meeting (55%). Science can help explain why the visual component has the most impact on first impressions.[18] The processing speed of vivid images with our eyes is twenty-five times faster than the processing speed of our listening capability. The old brain makes the primary first impression on visual information in less than a second—far before the auditory information arrives.

As you can see, how you look (dress, appearance, body language) is vital when you first meet someone. This is not fair, right? But that is the way it is, and since these facts about the brain have been around for several million years, it is not going to change anytime soon.

THE NEUROSCIENCE OF SELLING

Selling to Different Personality Types

It is difficult to sell to someone else unless you know their personality style and how it differs from your own. There are hundreds of personality assessments that have been developed over many years. Almost all of these assessments reduce us to one of four basic personality styles using two variables: ego drive and empathy. In the business-oriented Advanced Personality Questionnaire (APQ) system, developed by Dr. Larry Craft, these four types are called the **Driver**, the **Communicator**, the **Supporter**, and the **Thinker**.

A simple way to determine what type of personality style someone else has is to ask yourself (or your coach) two questions:

1 Are they fact- or feeling-oriented? (Empathy Level)

- Drivers and Thinkers are fact-oriented.

- Communicators and Supporters are feeling-oriented.

Four Types of Personality

	Low Empathy (task/fact oriented)	High Empathy (people/feeling oriented)
High Ego Drive (impatient, extrovert) (fast-paced)	**DIRECTIVE DRIVER** *Wants to:* **Beat the competition**	**EXPRESSIVE COMMUNICATOR** *Wants to:* **Get recognition and praise**
Low Ego Drive (patient, introvert) (slow-paced)	**REFLECTIVE THINKER** *Wants to:* **Improve business processes and results**	**SUPPORTIVE HELPER** *Wants to:* **Support others**

2 Are they fast- or slow-paced? (Ego Drive Level)

- Drivers and Communicators are fast-paced.
- Thinkers and Supporters are slow-paced.

The Drivers and Thinkers are in the two quadrants on the left side of the personality chart and have less empathy for others. When they get to work, they are all about tasks, facts, and getting the job done.

The Communicators and Supporters are in the two quadrants on the right side of the personality chart and have more empathy. When they get to work, they are all about rapport building, people issues, and teamwork.

The Drivers and Communicators are in the top two quadrants and have more ego drive. They are fast talking, fast thinking, and quick decision-makers. They are focused on the big picture.

The Thinkers and Supporters are in the bottom two quadrants and have less ego drive. They are slower paced, more cautious, and need more time to make decisions. The Thinkers want more data, and the Supporters want to collaborate with everyone in making the decision.

Elite salespeople have learned which personality style they are and how to adapt to sell to the other three personality styles at the expert level. The following are characteristics of what each of the four personality styles wants when they are considering a purchase.

When selling to Drivers, they want:

- *Little (if any) rapport building*
- *More big picture*
- *Fewer details, except for significant return on investment (ROI) for their business*

When selling to Thinkers, they want:

- *Little (if any) rapport building*
- *Less big picture*
- *More details, so they can take time to study and consider your solution*

When selling to Communicators, they want:

▸ *More rapport building at the start of the meeting*

▸ *More big picture, including stories about how your company has helped other companies just like theirs*

▸ *Fewer details, except for your experience with large and significant customers*

When selling to Supporters, they want:

▸ *More rapport building and may ease the discussion into family and friends*

▸ *Less big picture, except for stories of how your solutions can reduce risk*

▸ *More details that are helpful to them and provide the information they need to champion your solution within their company*

Elite salespeople understand that 75 percent of the rest of the people in the world likely have a different personality style than they do. Plus, the buyers with personalities diagonal from theirs on the quadrant

chart are far different (mismatched in both ego drive and empathy).

Multiple studies from the large sales institutes and emotional intelligence (EQ) training companies show that the success rate with buyers is 80 percent when you successfully match personality styles (send a Driver to sell to a Driver).

There is also an 80 percent success rate if you mirror

the buyer's style by giving them the information they need to make their buying decision according to their style, not what you would like to give based on your personality style. If you do not match or mirror the style and...

- *try to sell the Driver or Communicator on the details only,*
- *try to sell the Thinker or Supporter on the big picture only,*
- *fail to build rapport with the Communicator or Supporter, or*
- *try to robustly build rapport with the Driver or Thinker...*

...you have a 20 percent chance of making the sale; yet another clear example of the Pareto principle (80/20 rule).

Encourage the Buyer to Talk First

Smile, smile, smile. Devise an opening statement that gets the buyer to talk about what they like to talk about and engage Old Brain Activator #1—ME ME ME Focus. They feel good because they are talking about what they like to talk about, and they transfer that good feeling to you (Psychology 101). The *tone* of the meeting changes for the better.

In the next chapter, we will be doubling down on this methodology when we discuss how you as a salesperson can listen. However, the specific goal to focus on in this section and the next is that you need to get your customer talking. If they aren't talking, how can you listen and respond to their needs?

Here are some guidelines to get the buyer talking first and keeping it simple, supporting the second decision-making old brain activator: Simple, Easy-to-Grasp Ideas.

Make a statement about their interest and ask an open-ended question. Keep it focused on business,

professional, or technical items of interest to the buyer. Use personal items as the last resort, unless you have a strong, mutual personal interest (e.g., golf or French impressionist prints) or if your coach suggests that you use it.

Bring up topics in which you are knowledgeable or for which you have a genuine curiosity. Do not try to fake sincerity (it usually backfires). Stay away from words that are too flattering (terrific, outstanding, etc.) and always mention your coach.

Here is an example of how to put this advice to work:

"Good to meet you, Bob. I was just talking to Bill Smith, and he told me about the program you started to mentor young engineers here at AJAX. How did you get the program started?"

If you have nothing else, use his or her job.

"Good to meet you, Bob. It looks like you have a great job here at AJAX. How did you get started in this business?"

THE NEUROSCIENCE OF SELLING

Keep the Buyer Talking

Once the discussion shifts to business and the buyer asks about your company's offerings, respond with the Socratic opener.[19]

"I'm prepared to discuss our six different outsourcing solutions, but if you could give me your thoughts on your main interests first, then we can focus on our solutions that will be the best fit to help you. Could you tell me...?"

Or

"So that I can recommend the best solution, I would like to understand..."

This technique is called the Socratic opener, as it responds to the way the Greek philosopher Socrates taught. When a student would ask him a question, Socrates would respond with a question and keep asking the student questions until the student discovered the answer to their original question!

The Socratic opener has three great benefits:

1. You come across as respectful and polite by the way your question is posed.

2. It gets the buyer talking about their needs first.

3. It avoids having to start describing your capabilities. How many buyers want to listen to a thirty-minute, twenty-slide presentation about seven different IT solutions? (Hint: none! Well, maybe *some* of the Thinkers…)

CHAPTER

SIX

Perfect Listening

The best salespeople are not the great talkers—they are the great listeners. We find that the people most interesting to us are the people who are interested in us.

Buyers want to interact with salespeople who are sincerely interested in their needs, who ask great questions to thoroughly understand their needs, and who offer solutions that are perfectly tuned to their needs.

Four old brain activators apply here: ME ME ME Focus, Beginnings and Endings, Vivid Images, and Active Engagement. Five cognitive biases that were covered previously apply: Compliment, Likability, Safety, Trust, and Warmth. Here are three new biases that apply:

Listening Biases

The Action Bias

This bias demonstrates our tendency to think that value can only be realized through action. Simply put, we are happier doing anything, even if it is counterproductive, rather than doing nothing, even if doing nothing is the best course of action.

> **PRACTICAL APPLICATION**
>
> Remember that listening before you speak is doing something valuable. It is giving you vital buyer information that you would not have if you spent most of your time talking. Never interrupt a buyer who is speaking.

The Consistency Bias

We are biased to retroactively adjust our attitudes to avoid admitting to being changeable or wrong. We remember past attitudes and behaviors incorrectly in

order to reflect our current views. It leads us to think we are far more consistent than we actually are.

PRACTICAL APPLICATION

As you go through the sales process with a buyer, be consistent in what you say and do. Continually ask questions that elicit positive responses so the buyer maintains a positive state of mind.

The Rationale Bias

A rationale is a set of reasons or a logical basis for a course of action or a particular belief. We are much more likely to act when given a reason to do so.

> **PRACTICAL APPLICATION**
>
> After summarizing what the buyer tells you, ask, "Is there anything else I need to know?" and remain silent until they tell you. This simple question reminds their old brain of something they may have left out.
>
> These four old brain activators and many cognitive biases affect how we listen to the buyer. Knowing and understanding them allows you to become a perfect listener and help you help your buyers make the right decisions.

Three Steps to Perfect Listening

Most of us have good hearing, but most of us also can be bad listeners. We too often passively listen to respond, rather than actively listen to understand. Wouldn't you like to become a *perfect listener* like an elite salesperson? It requires active listening with a three-step technique:

1. Totally focus on the buyer's point of view.

2 Ask permission to take notes and take notes.

3 Summarize and repeat the buyer's needs back to them to get agreement.

1. Totally Focus on the Buyer's Point of View

To understand the buyer's needs, you need to focus on their perspective before you start offering solutions. This technique is extremely difficult to execute, because it is estimated that it only takes 20 percent of our brain to listen. The real question is: What is going on with the other 80 percent of our brain? We all know the answer. We can easily fall into the trap of thinking about other things: how to respond, our current business issues, the ball game last night, and personal issues.

In addition, as soon as we hear several buyer needs that match other jobs done for current customers, our pattern-matching old brain (Vivid Images activator) starts urging the hominid brain to talk about those offerings. This temptation is the action bias at work.

Ask questions to understand the buyer's needs. Based on years of continuous neuroscience research, we have learned that buyers value their conclusions and what they say *much* more than they value what they are told. Therefore, ask what their issues are and keep asking questions until you totally understand the customer's need.[20]

The Most Important Questions to Ask

1 You really know a lot about this situation. Could you expand on the details? (Compliment Bias)

2 Could you describe the buying decision process in your company?

3 Could you discuss the results you are looking for? (Old Brain Activator #6—Active Engagement)

4 Could you describe criteria that you will use to select a vendor?

2. Ask Permission to Take Notes and Take Notes

There are eight reasons to take notes:

1 It takes 80 percent of your brain to listen and process the information while writing it down, as opposed to 20 percent when you are not taking notes. So, while you are taking notes, it is much easier to resist talking and/or interrupting the buyer.

2 Taking notes communicates that you are actively listening. It lets the buyer know that their words are valuable enough to write down. (Likability Bias)

3 Based on neuroscience research, if you are with a stranger and not taking notes, you can only remember three main points within twenty minutes after the conversation is over.

4. It makes you appear like you are an interested, engaged professional, and this image causes buyers to take you more seriously. (Trust Bias)

5. It gives you the information to put into CRM so that the next person who talks to that buyer (whether it is you or someone else from your company) is totally up to speed with the information that the buyer has previously provided. (Trust Bias)

6. It slows the needs analysis process down, which gives the buyer more time to think and share. It also gives you more time to process the information and devise appropriate and relevant follow-up questions. (Trust Bias)

7. Writing down what you hear increases retention by 40 percent to 70 percent.

8   It reduces the anxiety most buyers feel when sales-people don't take notes. If you are not taking notes, buyers are worried that you will not be able to respond with a targeted proposal and therefore will totally waste their time. (Safety Bias)

Don't Forget That Part Where We Said to Ask Permission!

Elite salespeople do not just start taking notes. They ask permission for the following important reasons:

1   It is polite and shows respect. (Likability Bias)

2   It gives control of the conversation to the buyer. Once the buyer feels like they are in control, if they see you struggling to keep up, the buyer will slow down. (Old Brain Activator #1—ME ME ME Focus.) But actually, this is an illusion of control. Since you

are asking questions, you are guiding the conversation where you need it to go and you are extracting the information you need to determine if you can help the buyer. The listener is actually in control of the conversation.

3. It lets skeptical buyers know exactly what you are doing, and, as many of us have learned, many buyers are skeptical by nature or training or both. (Trust Bias)

4. You get your first *yes* in the staircase to yes (to the deal you want). Because of the consistency bias, the more yeses you get up front, the higher the probability of getting the yes to the deal you want. (Consistency Bias)

- Ask: Is it okay if I take notes? (Answer: Yes)

- Don't Ask: Do you mind if I take notes? (Answer: No!)

- 100% of the buyers will agree to let you take notes. Buyers WANT you to get it right.

Buyers do not want to interact with salespeople who do not take notes and offer solutions that are not the right fit and totally waste their time (Safety Bias). There are only three things in life that are 100%: death, taxes, and the percent of buyers who will agree to let sellers take notes!

3. Summarize and Repeat Back to the Buyer to Get Agreement

Just prior to offering solutions, summarize the buyer's requirements back to them. It is more important to summarize than repeat back verbatim, as it shows that you totally understand their needs.

Your summary results in one of two outcomes.

1. You have it exactly right, having a great impact on the buyer. You not only listened well, but you also must really understand. (Trust Bias)

2 You do not have it exactly right, allowing the buyer to correct you and help you avoid making the mistake of suggesting an offering that does not respond to the buyer's issue. (Trust Bias)

When you summarize the buyer's needs, most of the time you get even more information. The buyer now has a very high comfort level with you (Warmth, Trust, and Likability biases).

This additional information is almost always important (they want you to get the business or at least submit a competent proposal), and now you have converted the buyer from treating you as a stranger to becoming your incipient inside coach.

Here are typical things buyers will tell you as they listen to your summary (if they haven't told you already):

- *Information they forgot to tell you*
- *The priority of their requirements/specifications*
- *Information about the incumbent*

- *Information about your competition and what they are proposing*
- *Internal politics*
- *Their decision-making process*
- *Other buyers you need to talk to and their personality types*
- *Their time frame*
- *Their budget*

Since their comfort level is now so high, buyers may mention other opportunities: "Can your company also do this?"

Also, they may reveal what is in it for them personally. This could be the key to the sale. If they have not already told you what is in it for them personally, you can always ask this question: "If your company doesn't solve this issue, what are the implications for the company and for you?"

Once they share the implications for them personally, and if you show empathy and they feel the empathy, you are way closer to the sale (90 percent) (Trust and Warmth biases).

If you have used all the perfect listening techniques well, you have clarified the buyer's needs in their mind. To the buyer, the discussion feels like a total collaboration (Likability Bias).

CHAPTER

SEVEN

Closing the Deal

If you want to be successful in sales, you need to know how to close deals—get the buyer to say yes. As the late, great Zig Ziglar used to say: "Nothing happens until a sale is made." However, we now know that neuroscience plays more of an important role in closing deals than we previously thought.[21]

Three old brain activators apply: ME ME ME Focus; Simple, Easy-to-Grasp Ideas; and Vivid Images. Six cognitive biases that were covered previously apply:

Action, Choice Supportive, Primacy, Safety, Trust, and Ultimate Attribution. Here are four new ones that apply:

Four Final Biases

The Anchor Bias

The anchor bias is the tendency of relying too heavily on the initial or first information offered when making decisions and subsequent judgments.

PRACTICAL APPLICATION

1. If you can, always be the first company to present.

2. Do not reveal your price before describing your value.

The Bandwagon Bias

The bandwagon bias is a psychological phenomenon where people do something primarily because other people are doing it, regardless of their own beliefs, which they may ignore or override. The bandwagon effect has wide implications and is commonly seen in politics and consumer behavior.

> **PRACTICAL APPLICATION**
>
> Emphasize the wide adoption of your solution to buyers.

The Single Option Aversion Bias

Consumers who are initially offered only one option are more likely to continue searching for alternatives even when other options are later presented. If initially offered two similar options, they are much more likely to make a buying decision at that point.

> **PRACTICAL APPLICATION**
>
> Never make your first offer to the buyer just a single option.

The Scarcity Bias

The scarcity bias occurs when we place a higher value on an object that is scarce. Therefore, we falsely believe an item that is in short supply, high demand, or exists only within a small window of time is of higher value than it actually is.

PRACTICAL APPLICATION

Let buyers know when the availability of your popular offerings is limited or when they are being offered at a reduced rate for a period of time.

In addition, there are six closing principles that elite salespeople use to close deals faster.

Six Closing Principles

Closing Principle #1

You cannot close until the buyer is ready to agree to the deal.
If you try to close before the buyer is ready, it can come across as pushy and may kill the sale altogether.

In the buyer's old brain, the image of a pushy retail salesperson may flash up, and they will attach that image to the salesperson. The probability of making a sale to this buyer is now about 5 percent.

You can easily see how Old Brain Activator #5—Vivid Images, the safety bias (salespeople are not considered safe), and the primacy bias (first impressions) come into play.

Closing Principle #2

Most buyers will almost never close themselves, even when they are ready.
Once buyers decide to buy, they quickly become frustrated with sellers who do not recognize they are

ready (Action Bias). The window of opportunity to close the deal at this point is short. You only have a few minutes depending on the buyer's personality style:

► *Drivers and Motivators = a minute or two*

► *Thinkers and Supporters = a few more minutes*

If sellers are timid at the closing point, they have a 90 percent chance of losing the sale.

Closing Principle #3

The combination of the conversation and the buyer's body language tells you when the buyer is ready (buyer's shift).
There will come a time when your selling efforts overcome the buyer's anchor bias, and they decide they want your product or service. Watch and listen for signals that indicate the buyer has shifted (in some cases, a few of these signals can occur simultaneously).

You will get some verbal signals, including:

▸ *The buyer makes "attachment" statements: "This is a good location for the item."*

▸ *The buyer repeats a question: "Can you explain the response feature again?"*

▸ *The buyer asks risk-mitigation questions: "So, you said this comes with a guarantee?" (They want to make sure they cover their bases.)*

▸ *The buyer mentions an outside recommendation: "So, you said Bob is using your service and he says it's working well for him." (Buyers who seek recommendations are serious about buying.)*

▸ *The buyer relates unfavorable stories about specific competitors: "I had a problem when I used (insert company name) for a similar project." With reassurance that you are different, they are ready. (Old Brain Activator #4—Clear Distinction)*

▸ *The buyer asks you for personal details: "How long have you been with the organization?" (They are ready to buy the product and also need to buy you.)*

▸ *The buyer starts talking about the future: "Is a kickoff meeting a good idea?"*

You can see how Old Brain Activator #4—Clear Distinction and the bandwagon bias (lots of people are using us) come into play.

However, most of the signals are nonverbal.[22] Recall Dr. Mehrabian's communications study mentioned in chapter five. Body language provides 55 percent of the signals, which come from the old brain and are more revealing than verbal signals. Look at the following chart we developed and compare the body signals when the buyer has not shifted with the body signals when the buyer has shifted.

Once you start to observe the lack of tension in the buyer's body language, you will know they are relaxed and ready to hear a closing approach. If there's a disconnect between what they're saying and what their body says, remember that body language does not lie.

	BUYER HAS SHIFTED	BUYER HAS NOT SHIFTED
FACE	Friendly, smiling, slow head nod, pleasant expression, active	Furrowed brow, little change in expression, tense
ARMS	Uncrossed, taking jacket off	Tense, crossed, shoulders raised
EYES	Good eye contact, raising both eyebrows, eyes widening, pupils growing wider	Avoiding eye contact, looking at watch or clock, sideways glances
HANDS	Palms open, handling your material, rubbing hands together	Clasped, clenched, tense, fidgeting with objects, pushing on desk away from you, covering mouth while speaking
LEGS	Uncrossed or crossed towards you	Crossed at the ankles, crossed away from you, bouncing leg up and down, tapping foot
BODY ANGLE	Moving closer to you, on edge of chair	Slouching, hunched over, putting space between you, tense, turned away, leaning back in the chair

Closing Principle #4

Buyers want a definitive closing proposal.

Closing Principle #4 is the question posed by the sales-person to get the buyer to say yes and agree to the deal. Buyers do not want a two-paragraph closing approach. They want it to be clear what you are asking for (Old Brain Activator #2—Simple, Easy-to-Grasp Ideas).

Here are six classic techniques to close the sale in Principle #4:

- *Closing Technique No. 1—The Direct Close: "Linda, it looks like we've got a nice match between what you need and what we are offering. We can have your call center up and running in about six weeks. The cost is $120,000 per year. Would you like to go ahead with this project?" (Old Brain Activator #2—Simple, Easy-to-Grasp Ideas)*

- *Closing Technique No. 2—The Alternative Close: "Bob, would you like to start with the one- or*

two-day training seminar for your salespeople?" *(Single Option Aversion Bias)*

▸ *Closing Technique No. 3—The "I Recommend" Close: "In order to add this functionality to your augmented reality system, we'll need a contract modification of about $20,000.* **I recommend that** *we get started right away in order to meet your schedule.* **Are you ready to go ahead with this, Joe?"** *This closing technique is used with current customers who know and trust you. Whatever you recommend, they will agree to. (Trust Bias)*

▸ *Closing Technique No. 4—The "When or If" Close: "So,* **if we don't** *include Global Positioning System functionality into our solution, your avionics upgrade package will lag behind the competition.* **Would you like to include it?"** *(Rationale Bias)*

▸ *Closing Technique No. 5—The "Test It Out First" Close: "We have five hundred customers using this tool. We will be happy to provide your sales manager with a free subscription to Crystal Knows for one month on a trial basis.* **Would you like to start at the end of the month?"** *(Bandwagon Bias)*

▸ *Closing Technique No. 6—The Window of Opportunity Close: "The next quarterly computer simulation training class starts on November 5. This class is filling up quickly.* **If you want to get your three engineers in this training, I suggest you make a commitment today. Are you ready to sign them up?"** *(Scarcity Bias)*

Closing Principle #5

After you ask for the business, say nothing until the buyer responds.

You want the buyer to say "Yes," "No," or "No, because …" (the objection you've been looking for). Whoever speaks next "owns the product."

In many cases, buyers need to think about your proposal before they decide. They may be having thoughts like: *How does this offering compare to the other three competitors'? Can we afford this capital outlay right now? Will the bank support the project? Our team has a lot of projects on our plate right now. Do we have the ability to take on this project and do a good job?*

Don't interrupt their thinking! Don't fall prey to the action bias (any action is better than no action).

If you do, they are no longer *thinking* about your offer. Be quiet and perfectly still (don't distract the buyer). If you do interrupt the buyer, it comes across as threatening (safety bias); also, trust is lost (trust bias). The probability of making the sale has now plummeted to 5 percent.

Closing Principle #6

After the deal is done, stop talking!

The best way to *unsell* a closed deal is to keep talking about it (action bias). The buyer may discover some aspect of your offering that needs further discussion (Ouch!). For example, you might say, "Thanks. This will be great! It will be our first CRM implementation in a large manufacturing company like yours." (The buyer groans!)

Instead, immediately congratulate the buyer on their great decision (choice-supportive bias). Shift the discussion to sports, weather, news—anything.

All customer-interfacing people need to be trained to stop talking at this point. Buyers are busy—it is time to go!

Elite salespeople have learned these six neuroscience-based principles on how to close deals. Now that you know them, you can close deals faster and at a higher confidence level. So go out there and sell something!

Conclusion

I believe reading and learning are key factors in having both a rewarding personal life and a successful professional life. The hard part is taking what has been learned, applying it, and creating new and positive habits.

Creating new habits sounds easy, but it really isn't. Most research in this area tells us that it takes thirty-plus days of sustained effort, practice, and trial and error to get a new habit ingrained in our behavior!

The first thing to do is to identify habits that you want to turn into behaviors. On the following pages, I have listed some potential action items that you

THE NEUROSCIENCE OF SELLING

might consider adopting to improve your salesman-ship capabilities. Check off the ones you think would make the biggest improvement in your near-term sales results.

Then pick your top three action items and work on them consistently for a month. Once those are engrained, work on the next three action items on your list. I believe you'll be amazed at how much better you will be at sales, how much more you will enjoy selling, and how much more successful you will be in your career.

If you would like more information on the neuro-science of selling, want to watch short reinforcement videos, read blogs, listen to podcasts, take a sales aptitude assessment, or attend public sales training days, visit our website at www.asherstrategies.com.

NEXT
STEPS

Potential Action Items

- ▶ *Develop a qualification process for new leads.*

- ▶ *Activate the Sales Navigator tool on LinkedIn and learn how to use it to identify new prospects, research buyers, and find potential inside coaches.*

- ▶ *Rework your company presentations, proposals, and websites to include the six old brain activators.*

- ▶ *Take a sales aptitude assessment to know and understand your personal selling style and learn how to sell to other personality styles.*

▸ *Create a story that you can share with prospects regarding how you helped a customer with the same or similar problem and saved them time and money.*

▸ *Research buyers using social media (e.g., LinkedIn) to obtain information so that you can easily motivate them to talk first.*

▸ *When interacting with a prospect for the first time, compliment them early about a video you watched on their website, their company's reputation, their facilities, etc.*

▸ *Give the prospect a gift with every interaction (a book, report, prop, link to an educational video, link to a new website, etc.).*

▸ *If possible, always be the first to present.*

▸ *Always offer the prospect two or three options; never only one or more than three.*

▸ *Use the six closing techniques to develop scripts tailored to your customer's situation.*

Notes

1   Andy Wai Kan Yeung, Tazuko K. Goto, and W. Keung Leung, "The Changing Landscape of Neuroscience Research, 2006–2015: A Bibliometric Study," *Frontiers in Neuroscience* 11 (March 2017), https://doi.org/10.3389/fnins.2017.00120.

2   fMRI is based on the same technology as magnetic resonance imaging (MRI)—a noninvasive test that uses a strong magnetic field and radio waves to create detailed images of the body—but instead of creating images of organs and tissues like MRI, fMRI looks at blood flow in the brain to detect areas of activity. See https://science.howstuffworks.com/fmri.htm.

3   In the 1960s, American neuroscientist Paul MacLean formulated the triune brain model—the division of the human brain into three distinct regions organized into a hierarchy based on an evolutionary view of brain development. See Andreas Komnios, "The Concept of the Triune Brain," Interaction Design Foundation, https://www.interaction-design.org/literature/article/the-concept-of-the-triune-brain.

4   Patrick Renvoise and Christophe Morin, in their 2002 book *Neuromarketing*,

were among the first to point to old brain "triggers." These were mainly thought of only as a tool for marketing. They apply to sales as well.

5   A great resource for understanding more about cognitive processes is Daniel Kahneman's 2011 book, *Thinking, Fast and Slow*.

6   These are the selling skills where the old brain activators and cognitive biases have the most impact. They are part of my top ten selling skills that I developed for ASHER sales training courses and are fully explained in my first book, *Close Deals Faster*.

7   Harvard fMRI research on how disclosing information can affect the brain can be found in David Hoffeld's 2016 book *The Science of Selling*.

8   Victoria Woollaston, "Why Talking About Yourself with Friends Can Be as Pleasurable as Sex," *Daily Mail*, July 18, 2013, https://www.dailymail.co.uk /sciencetech/article-2368451/Why-talking-friends-pleasurable-SEX.html.

9   Jack Norris, "Trade Show Graphics—You Have 3 Quick Seconds to Be Victorious," https://american-image.com/trade-show-graphics-you-have-3 -quick-seconds-to-be-victorious/.

10 Martin Lindstrom, *Buyology: Truth and Lies About Why We Buy* (New York: Doubleday, 2008), 11–12.

11 Dan Ariely, in his 2008 book *Predictably Irrational: The Hidden Forces That Shape Our Decisions*, gives easy-to-understand examples of cognitive biases that challenge assumptions about rational thought in decision-making.

12 My top ten selling skills as listed in *Close Deals Faster*: 1. Focus on a Few Top Prospects; 2. Thoroughly Research Prospects and Their Organizations Prior to First Contact; 3. Use Insiders to Fully Understand Prospects and Their Requirements; 4. Sell Yourself by Building Rapport; 5. Ask the Right Questions, Listen, and Guide the Conversation; 6. Use Powerful Marketing

Messages; 7. Act as a Business Consultant and Expertly Handle Objections; 8. Recognize When the Buyer is Ready to Buy (Buyer's Shift) and Know How to Close the Sale; 9. Build Long-Term Relationships with the New Customers; and 10. Ask for Referrals.

13   Many sales experts have come to this same conclusion, including: Grant Cardone, "Your Survival Depends on Following Up on Internet Leads—Fast," *Entrepreneur*, August 29, 2014, https://www.entrepreneur.com /article/236916; Jaime Paredes, "12 Touches to Close a Deal," Entergage Videos, https://www.entergagevideos.com/12-touches-close-deal/, accessed March 2, 2019; Caroline Japic, "The New B2B Marketing Reality: More Touches Are Required to Close the Deal," *Forbes*, August 7, 2017, https://www.forbes.com/sites/forbescommunicationscouncil/2017/08/07 /the-new-b2b-marketing-reality-more-touches-are-required-to-close -the-deal/#1a300a7621b2; Mike Brooks, "Following Up with Prospects: 90 Percent Never Do," SalesGravey, https://www.salesgravy.com/sales -articles/closing-techniques/Following-Up-with-Prospects-90-Percent -Never-Do, accessed March 2, 2019.

14   Laurie Beasley, "Why It Takes 7 to 13+ Touches to Deliver a Qualified Sales Lead (Part 1)," Online Marketing Institute, October 10, 2013, https://www .onlinemarketinginstitute.org/blog/2013/10/why-it-takes-7-to-13-touches -to-deliver-a-qualified-sales-lead-part1/.

15   Tim Asimos, "3 Ways to Engage B2B Buyers Before They Engage You," circlesstudio.com, April 7, 2015, https://www.circlesstudio.com/blog/3 -ways-to-engage-b2b-buyers-before-they-engage-you/.

16   Sujan Patel, "5 Tips for Getting Your Cold-Sales Emails Read," *Entrepreneur*, September 6, 2018, https://www.entrepreneur.com/article/319528.

17   Daniela Schiller, Jonathan Freeman, Jason Mitchell, James Uleman, and

Elizabeth Phelps, "A Neural Mechanism of First Impressions," *Nature Neuroscience* 12 (2009): 501–514; Eric Wargo, "How Many Seconds to a First Impression?" *Observer*, July 2006, https://www.psychologicalscience .org/observer/how-many-seconds-to-a-first-impression.

18   A good read about body language impact on first impressions: Patti Wood, *Snap: Making the Most of First Impressions, Body Language, and Charisma* (Novato, California: New World Library, 2012).

19   Kevin Daley, *Socratic Selling: How to Ask the Questions That Get the Sale* (New York: McGraw-Hill Education, 1995).

20   Jeb Blunt, "Do You Listen to Me?" in *Sales EQ: How Ultra-High Performers Leverage Sales-Specific Emotional Intelligence to Close the Complex Deal* (Hoboken: John Wiley & Sons, 2017): 197–204.

21   The following book chapter gives additional background as to why this is so: David Hoffeld, "Closing Redefined: Obtaining Strategic Commitments" in *The Science of Selling: Proven Strategies to Make Your Pitch, Influence Decisions, and Close the Deal* (New York: Penguin Random House, 2016): 5–8.

22   The original *Body Language* book was written by Julius Fast in the 1960s. A very detailed and popular book today is: Joe Navarro, *What Every BODY Is Saying: An Ex-FBI Agent's Guide to Speed-Reading People* (New York: William Morrow, 2008).

In his first career, **John Asher** was captain of two nuclear-powered fast attack submarines. In his final job in the U.S. Navy, he was the program manager of a billion-dollar software development program. A lot of what he learned about leadership and sales he learned in the U.S. Navy.

In John's second career, he cofounded an engineering company that grew at a 42 percent per year growth rate compounded for fourteen straight years. Along the way, the firm acquired seven other companies, and John gained key insights into what it takes to develop a fast-growing business where everybody in the company is in sales!

In his third career, John started a sales and marketing advisory business to share the lessons he learned from being on the front lines of selling complex products and services for over twenty years. Those lessons were translated into his top ten selling skills that are the blocking and tackling of successful sales. He and his team have trained over seventy thousand salespeople in twenty-two countries on his efficient and effective sales process to quickly close new business.

John is a managing director of the Business Growth Alliance and is also a special advisor to the private equity divisions of Goldman Sachs and Indian Rivers Advisors.

Over the last two decades, John has mentored a

large cadre of speakers and trainers that has fueled the growth of ASHER.

John is a recent recipient of the Lifetime Speaker Achievement Award for extraordinary contributions to Vistage, an international organization of CEOs. His first book, *Close Deals Faster*, is an award winner in the business sales category of the 2018 International Book Awards.

NEW! Only from Simple Truths®

IGNITE READS
spark impact in just one hour

IGNITE READS IS A NEW SERIES OF 1-HOUR READS WRITTEN BY WORLD-RENOWNED EXPERTS!

These captivating books will help you become the best version of yourself, allowing for new opportunities in your personal and professional life. Accelerate your career and expand your knowledge with these powerful books written on today's hottest ideas.

TRENDING BUSINES AND PERSONAL GROWTH TOPICS

 Read in an hour or less

 Leading experts and authors

 Bold design and captivating conte